american popular piano

SKILLS

4

T0084325

Created by
Dr. Scott
McBride Smith

Series Composer
Christopher
Norton

Editor
Dr. Scott
McBride Smith

Associate Editor
Clarke
MacIntosh

NV Music

Book Design & Engraving
Andrew Jones

Cover Design
Wagner Design

Introduction

Everyone agrees that Tiger Woods is one of the greatest golfers of all time. Some even think he is the best ever! He won the 1997 Masters Tournament when he was 21 years old, the youngest winner in history. He was also the youngest golfer to complete a career *Grand Slam*, winning all four major championships by the age of 25.

How did he do it? Let's see what he says.

From early childhood I dreamed of being the world's best golfer. I worked hard and applied my family's values to everything I did. Integrity, honesty, discipline, responsiblity and fun; I learned these values at home and in school, each one pushing me further toward my dream.

Eldrick (Tiger) Woods
Letter from Tiger, Tiger Woods Foundation Website
http://www.twfound.org

The best way to achieve [a] goal is through sound fundamentals.

Tiger Woods
Golf Digest, November 1998

What's your dream? Do you want to be one of the world's best musicians? play piano for your own enjoyment? or entertain your friends and family? No matter which, Tiger is right. Hard work, responsibility – and fun! – will be the keystones to your success.

In golf, the term "fundamentals" covers many things. In piano playing, we can break it down into three broad groupings.

- **Technic.** This is the ability to readily make the motions that create beautiful sounds. Dynamic control, tonal evenness and variety, and speed would fall into this category.
- **Sightreading.** You might also call these "quick learning" skills. Seeing patterns, noticing details, and playing without stopping – right away.
- **Listening.** This is perhaps the most important of all! If you can't hear the sounds of a piece in your mind before you play, you will never do a good job performing it. Psychologists call this "audiation".

Do you think practicing basic skills is boring? Get over it!

Your playing will never be as good or as enjoyable as you want it to be if your basic skills are not excellent. Every athlete – including Tiger – spends time on drills, exercises and warm-ups outside of the game. Pianists should, too. When your piano fundamentals become strong, you will learn everything more easily and perform more confidently.

This book is designed to help, but it won't work if you don't! Practice carefully and frequently. Spend some time every day on your basic skills and, who knows ... you may become the Tiger Woods of the piano.

Library and Archives Canada Cataloguing in Publication

Smith, Scott McBride

American popular piano [music] : skills / created by Scott McBride Smith ;
series composer, Christopher Norton ;
editor, Scott McBride Smith ; associate editor, Clarke MacIntosh.

To be complete in 11 volumes.
Publisher's nos.: APP S-00 (level P); APP S-01 (level 1); APP S-02 (level 2).
Contents: Preparatory level -- Level 1 -- Level 2.
Miscellaneous information: The series is organized in 11 levels, from preparatory to level 10, each including a repertoire album, an etudes album, a skills book, a "technic" book, and an instrumental backings compact disc.

ISBN 978-1-897379-22-6 (preparatory level).--ISBN 978-1-897379-23-3 (level 1).--
ISBN 978-1-897379-24-0 (level 2).--ISBN 978-1-897379-25-7 (level 3).--
ISBN 978-1-897379-26-4 (level 4).--ISBN 978-1-897379-27-1 (level 5)

1. Piano--Studies and exercises. 2. Piano--Studies and exercises--Juvenile.
I. Norton, Christopher, 1953- II. MacIntosh, S. Clarke, 1959- III. Title.

LEVEL 4 SKILLS

Table of Contents

Unit One - Module One

A. Technic

Set weekly practice schedule as assigned by your teacher. For directions, see *How to Use This Book* on page 50.

1) Chords (pages 44-45)

No.(s) _____ ;

M.M. ♩ = _____ ;

key(s): F B♭ E♭ a

2) Arpeggios (page 46)

No.(s) _____ ;

M.M. ♩ = _____ ;

key(s): D A E

3) Blues Scales (page 47)

No.(s) _____ ;

M.M. ♩ = _____ ;

key(s): C G D

4) Drills (pages 48-49)

No.(s) _____ ;

M.M. ♩ = _____ ;

key(s): E B

5) Scales (pages 42-43)

No.(s) _____ ;

M.M. ♩ = _____ ;

key(s): F B♭ E♭ a

Articulation:

    legato   *staccato*   *portato*

Dynamic:

    f   *p*   *mf*   *mp*   *ff*   *pp*

Dynamic Variant

    < to top,   > to bottom

Articulation Variant

    left hand *legato* — right hand *staccato*

Rhythmic Variant

B. Prepared Sightreading Piece

Play at least three times each week. Keep a steady beat.

For directions, see *How to Use This Book* on page 50.

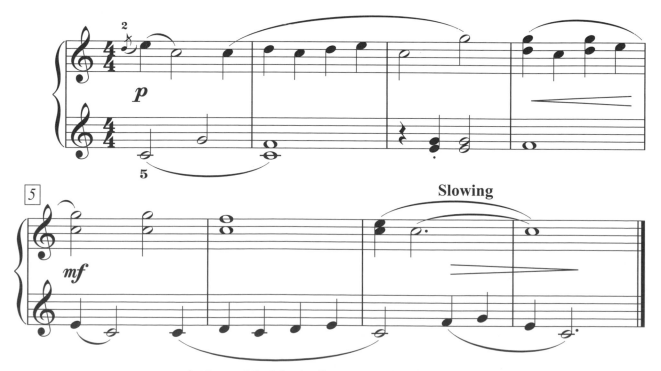

Slowing

C. Aural Skills - Rhythmic   For directions, see *How to Use This Book* on page 50.

Tap each exercise with the backing track to *Waltz of Regret* while counting out loud.
- start with the Practice track, progress to the Performance track
- count an ♪ pulse "1 - & - 2 - & - 3 - &" out

loud as you tap:
- i) First tap the lower rhythm on your left thigh.
- ii) Then tap the top rhythm on your right thigh.
- iii) Finally tap both rhythms, hands together.

D. Aural Skills - Pitch   For directions, see *How to Use This Book* on page 50.

1) a) Play the ♩ part at the piano while singing the ♩ part. Identify each interval: size – 1, 2, 3, 4, or 5; and quality – M (major), m (minor), or P (perfect).

b) Play the cadence. Then sing the top part while playing the bass line.

2) Sing and play the phrase simultaneously. Repeat, but don't play the last two bars – just sing them. Finally, just sing the entire phrase.

Unit One - Module Two

A. Technic

Set weekly practice schedule as assigned by your teacher. For directions, see *How to Use This Book* on page 50.

1) Chords (pages 44-45)

No.(s) _____ ;

M.M. ♩ = _____ ;

key(s): F B♭ E♭ a

2) Arpeggios (page 46)

No.(s) _____ ;

M.M. ♩ = _____ ;

key(s): D A E

3) Blues Scales (page 47)

No.(s) _____ ;

M.M. ♩ = _____ ;

key(s): C G D

4) Drills (pages 48-49)

No.(s) _____ ;

M.M. ♩ = _____ ;

key(s): E B

5) Scales (pages 42-43)

No.(s) _____ ;

M.M. ♩ = _____ ;

key(s): F B♭ E♭ a

Articulation:

   legato   *staccato*   *portato*

Dynamic:

   f   *p*   *mf*   *mp*   *ff*   *pp*

Dynamic Variant

>   to top,   <   to bottom

Articulation Variant

   left hand *legato* — right hand *staccato*

Rhythmic Variant

B. Prepared Sightreading Piece

Play at least three times each week. Keep a steady beat.

For directions, see *How to Use This Book* on page 50.

C. Aural Skills - Rhythmic   For directions, see *How to Use This Book* on page 50.

Tap each exercise with the backing track to *Ready for Action* while counting out loud.
- start with the Practice track, progress to the Performance track
- count an ♪ pulse "1 - & - 2 - & - 3 - & - 4 - &"

out loud as you tap:
- i)   First tap the lower rhythm on your left thigh.
- ii) Then tap the top rhythm on your right thigh.
- iii) Finally tap both rhythms, hands together.

a)

b)

c)

D. Aural Skills - Pitch   For directions, see *How to Use This Book* on page 50.

1) a) Play the ♩ part at the piano while singing the ♩ part.
Identify each interval: size – 1, 2, 3, 4, or 5; and quality – M (major), m (minor), or P (perfect).

b) Play the cadence. Then sing the top part while playing the bass line.

2) Sing and play the phrase simultaneously. Repeat, but don't play the last two bars – just sing them. Finally, just sing the entire phrase.

Unit One - Module Three

A. Technic

Set weekly practice schedule as assigned by your teacher. For directions, see *How to Use This Book* on page 50.

1) Chords (pages 44-45)

No.(s) _____ ;

M.M. ♩ = _____ ;

key(s): F B♭ E♭ a

2) Arpeggios (page 46)

No.(s) _____ ;

M.M. ♩ = _____ ;

key(s): D A E

3) Blues Scales (page 47)

No.(s) _____ ;

M.M. ♩ = _____ ;

key(s): C G D

4) Drills (pages 48-49)

No.(s) _____ ;

M.M. ♩ = _____ ;

key(s): E B

5) Scales (pages 42-43)

No.(s) _____ ;

M.M. ♩ = _____ ;

key(s): F B♭ E♭ a

Articulation:

  legato   staccato   portato

Dynamic:

  𝒇   𝒑   𝓂𝒇   𝓂𝓅   𝒇𝒇   𝓅𝓅

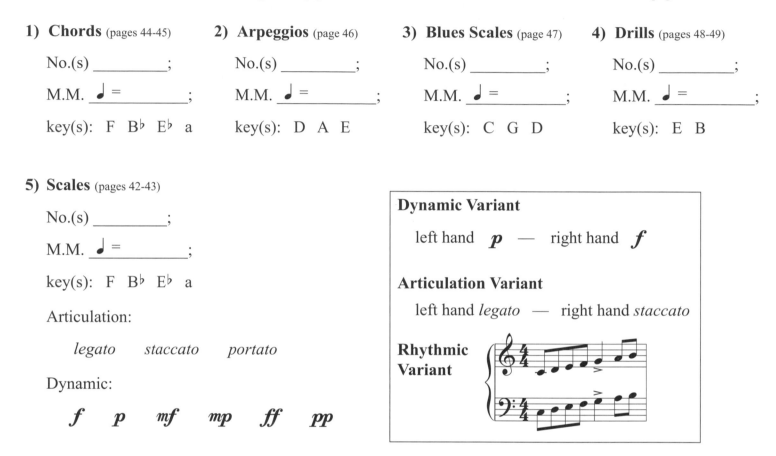

Dynamic Variant

  left hand 𝒑 — right hand 𝒇

Articulation Variant

  left hand *legato* — right hand *staccato*

Rhythmic Variant

B. Prepared Sightreading Piece

Play at least three times each week. Keep a steady beat.

For directions, see *How to Use This Book* on page 50.

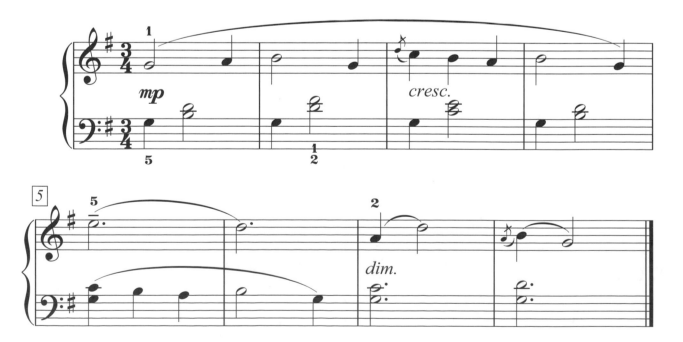

C. Aural Skills - Rhythmic For directions, see *How to Use This Book* on page 50.

Tap each exercise with the backing track to *Trucking Along* while counting out loud.
- start with the Practice track, progress to the Performance track
- count a swung ♪ pulse "1 - a - 2 - a - 3 - a - 4 - a"

out loud as you tap:
  i) First tap the lower rhythm on your left thigh.
  ii) Then tap the top rhythm on your right thigh.
  iii) Finally tap both rhythms, hands together.

a)

b)

c)

D. Aural Skills - Pitch For directions, see *How to Use This Book* on page 50.

1) a) Play the 𝅗𝅥 part at the piano while singing the 𝅘𝅥 part. Identify each interval: size – 1, 2, 3, 4, or 5; and quality – M (major), m (minor), or P (perfect).

b) Play the cadence. Then sing the top part while playing the bass line.

2) Sing and play the phrase simultaneously. Repeat, but don't play the last two bars – just sing them. Finally, just sing the entire phrase.

Unit One - Module Four

A. Technic

Set weekly practice schedule as assigned by your teacher. For directions, see *How to Use This Book* on page 50.

1) Chords (pages 44-45)

No.(s) _____ ;

M.M. ♩ = _____ ;

key(s): F B♭ E♭ a

2) Arpeggios (page 46)

No.(s) _____ ;

M.M. ♩ = _____ ;

key(s): D A E

3) Blues Scales (page 47)

No.(s) _____ ;

M.M. ♩ = _____ ;

key(s): C G D

4) Drills (pages 48-49)

No.(s) _____ ;

M.M. ♩ = _____ ;

key(s): E B

5) Scales (pages 42-43)

No.(s) _____ ;

M.M. ♩ = _____ ;

key(s): F B♭ E♭ a

Articulation:

    legato   *staccato*   *portato*

Dynamic:

    f   *p*   *mf*   *mp*   *ff*   *pp*

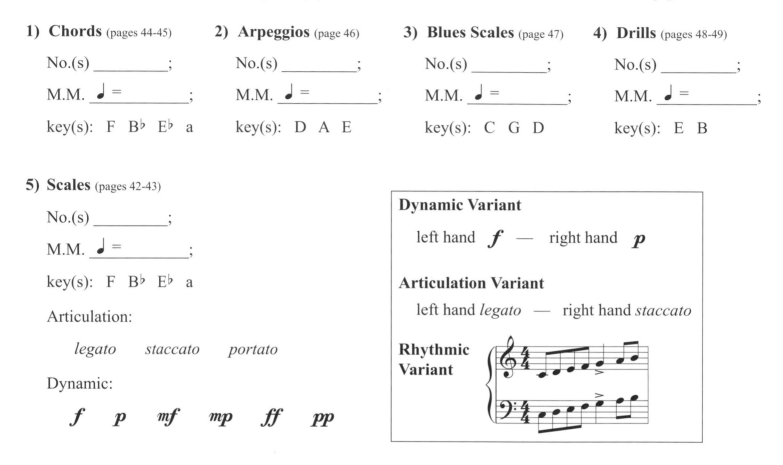

Dynamic Variant

left hand *f* — right hand *p*

Articulation Variant

left hand *legato* — right hand *staccato*

Rhythmic Variant

B. Prepared Sightreading Piece

Play at least three times each week. Keep a steady beat.

For directions, see *How to Use This Book* on page 50.

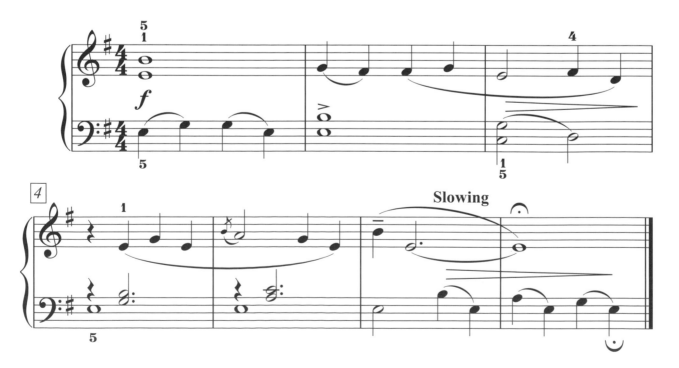

C. Aural Skills - Rhythmic   For directions, see *How to Use This Book* on page 50.

Tap each exercise with the backing track to *Rockin'
in the Aisles* while counting out loud.
- start with the Practice track, progress to the
  Performance track
- count an ♪ pulse "1 - & - 2 - & - 3 - & - 4 - &"

out loud as you tap:
- i)   First tap the lower rhythm on your left thigh.
- ii) Then tap the top rhythm on your right thigh.
- iii) Finally tap both rhythms, hands together.

a)

b)

c)

D. Aural Skills - Pitch   For directions, see *How to Use This Book* on page 50.

1) a) Play the ♩ part at the piano while singing the ♩ part.
   Identify each interval: size – 1, 2, 3, 4, or 5; and
   quality – M (major), m (minor), or P (perfect).

   b) Play the cadence. Then sing the top
   part while playing the bass line.

2) Sing and play the phrase simultaneously. Repeat, but don't play the last two bars – just sing them.
   Finally, just sing the entire phrase.

Unit Two - Module One

A. Technic

Set weekly practice schedule as assigned by your teacher. For directions, see *How to Use This Book* on page 50.

1) Chords (pages 44-45)

No.(s) _____ ;

M.M. ♩ = _____ ;

key(s): E♭ a e E

2) Arpeggios (page 46)

No.(s) _____ ;

M.M. ♩ = _____ ;

key(s): A E g

3) Blues Scales (page 47)

No.(s) _____ ;

M.M. ♩ = _____ ;

key(s): G D A

4) Drills (pages 48-49)

No.(s) _____ ;

M.M. ♩ = _____ ;

key(s): e b

5) Scales (pages 42-43)

No.(s) _____ ;

M.M. ♩ = _____ ;

key(s): E♭ a e E

Articulation:

   legato   *staccato*   *portato*

Dynamic:

   f   *p*   *mf*   *mp*   *ff*   *pp*

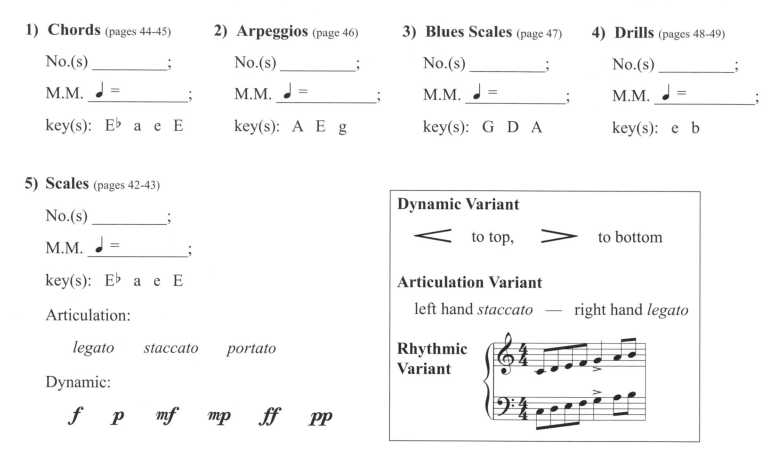

Dynamic Variant

< to top, > to bottom

Articulation Variant

left hand *staccato* — right hand *legato*

Rhythmic Variant

B. Prepared Sightreading Piece

For directions, see *How to Use This Book* on page 50.

Play at least three times each week. Keep a steady beat.

C. Aural Skills - Rhythmic   For directions, see *How to Use This Book* on page 50.

Tap each exercise with the backing track to *Trucking Along* while counting out loud.
- start with the Practice track, progress to the Performance track
- count a swung ♪ pulse "1 - a - 2 - a - 3 - a - 4 - a"

out loud as you tap:
- i)   First tap the lower rhythm on your left thigh.
- ii) Then tap the top rhythm on your right thigh.
- iii) Finally tap both rhythms, hands together.

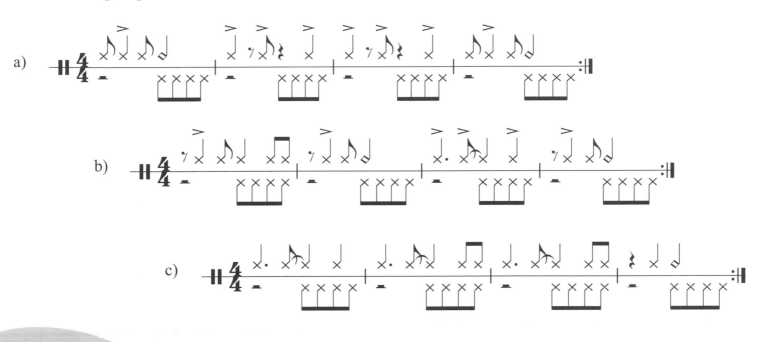

D. Aural Skills - Pitch   For directions, see *How to Use This Book* on page 50.

1) a) Play the ♩ part at the piano while singing the ♩ part. Identify each interval: size – 1, 2, 3, 4, or 5; and quality – M (major), m (minor), or P (perfect).

b) Play the cadence. Then sing the top part while playing the bass line.

2) Sing and play the phrase simultaneously. Repeat, but don't play the last two bars – just sing them. Finally, just sing the entire phrase.

Unit Two - Module Two

A. Technic

Set weekly practice schedule as assigned by your teacher. For directions, see *How to Use This Book* on page 50.

1) Chords (pages 44-45)

No.(s) _____ ;

M.M. ♩ = _____ ;

key(s): E♭ a e E

2) Arpeggios (page 46)

No.(s) _____ ;

M.M. ♩ = _____ ;

key(s): A E g

3) Blues Scales (page 47)

No.(s) _____ ;

M.M. ♩ = _____ ;

key(s): G D A

4) Drills (pages 48-49)

No.(s) _____ ;

M.M. ♩ = _____ ;

key(s): e b

5) Scales (pages 42-43)

No.(s) _____ ;

M.M. ♩ = _____ ;

key(s): E♭ a e E

Articulation:

legato   staccato   portato

Dynamic:

f   p   mf   mp   ff   pp

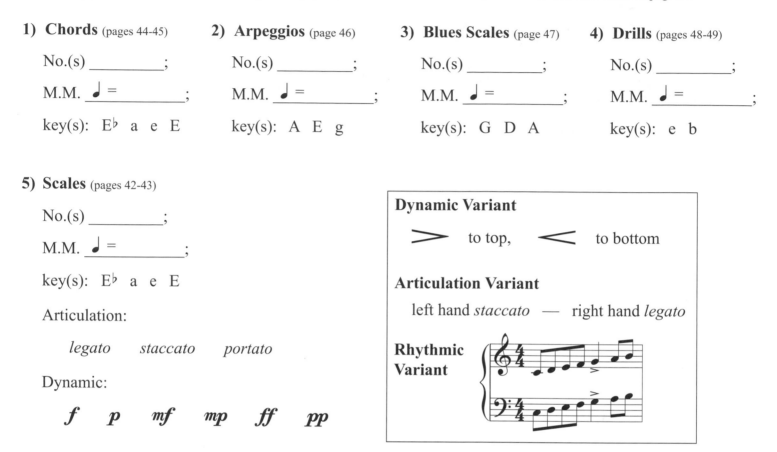

B. Prepared Sightreading Piece

For directions, see *How to Use This Book* on page 50.

Play at least three times each week. Keep a steady beat.

C. Aural Skills - Rhythmic For directions, see *How to Use This Book* on page 50.

Tap each exercise with the backing track to *Ready for Action* while counting out loud.
- start with the Practice track, progress to the Performance track
- count an ♪ pulse "1 - & - 2 - & - 3 - & - 4 - &"

out loud as you tap:
- i) First tap the lower rhythm on your left thigh.
- ii) Then tap the top rhythm on your right thigh.
- iii) Finally tap both rhythms, hands together.

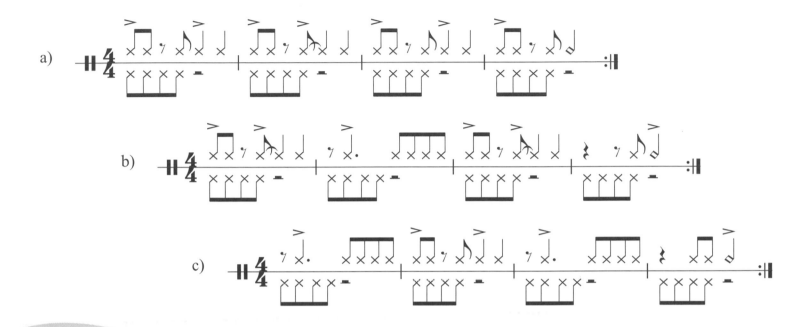

D. Aural Skills - Pitch For directions, see *How to Use This Book* on page 50.

1) a) Play the ♩ part at the piano while singing the ♩ part. Identify each interval: size – 1, 2, 3, 4, or 5; and quality – M (major), m (minor), or P (perfect).

b) Play the cadence. Then sing the top part while playing the bass line.

2) Sing and play the phrase simultaneously. Repeat, but don't play the last two bars – just sing them. Finally, just sing the entire phrase.

Unit Two - Module Three

A. Technic

Set weekly practice schedule as assigned by your teacher. For directions, see *How to Use This Book* on page 50.

1) Chords (pages 44-45)

No.(s) _____ ;

M.M. ♩ = _____ ;

key(s): E♭ a e E

2) Arpeggios (page 46)

No.(s) _____ ;

M.M. ♩ = _____ ;

key(s): A E g

3) Blues Scales (page 47)

No.(s) _____ ;

M.M. ♩ = _____ ;

key(s): G D A

4) Drills (pages 48-49)

No.(s) _____ ;

M.M. ♩ = _____ ;

key(s): e b

5) Scales (pages 42-43)

No.(s) _____ ;

M.M. ♩ = _____ ;

key(s): E♭ a e E

Articulation:

　　legato　　*staccato*　　*portato*

Dynamic:

　　𝆏 𝆏 *mf* *mp* *ff* *pp*

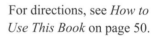

Dynamic Variant

　　left hand *p* — right hand *f*

Articulation Variant

　　left hand *staccato* — right hand *legato*

Rhythmic Variant

B. Prepared Sightreading Piece

Play at least three times each week. Keep a steady beat.

For directions, see *How to Use This Book* on page 50.

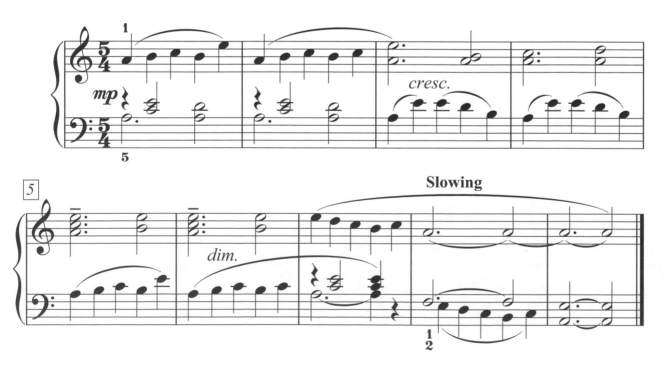

C. Aural Skills - Rhythmic
For directions, see *How to Use This Book* on page 50.

Tap each exercise with the backing track to *Waltz of Regret* while counting out loud.
- start with the Practice track, progress to the Performance track
- count an ♪ pulse "1 - & - 2 - & - 3 - &" out

loud as you tap:
- i) First tap the lower rhythm on your left thigh.
- ii) Then tap the top rhythm on your right thigh.
- iii) Finally tap both rhythms, hands together.

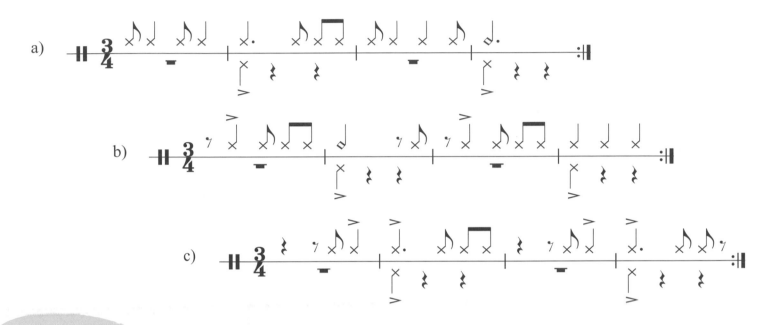

D. Aural Skills - Pitch
For directions, see *How to Use This Book* on page 50.

1) a) Play the ♩ part at the piano while singing the ♩ part. Identify each interval: size – 1, 2, 3, 4, or 5; and quality – M (major), m (minor), or P (perfect).

b) Play the cadence. Then sing the top part while playing the bass line.

2) Sing and play the phrase simultaneously. Repeat, but don't play the last two bars – just sing them. Finally, just sing the entire phrase.

Unit Two - Module Four

A. Technic

Set weekly practice schedule as assigned by your teacher. For directions, see *How to Use This Book* on page 50.

1) Chords (pages 44-45)

No.(s) _____;

M.M. ♩ = _____;

key(s): E♭ a e E

2) Arpeggios (page 46)

No.(s) _____;

M.M. ♩ = _____;

key(s): A E g

3) Blues Scales (page 47)

No.(s) _____;

M.M. ♩ = _____;

key(s): G D A

4) Drills (pages 48-49)

No.(s) _____;

M.M. ♩ = _____;

key(s): e b

5) Scales (pages 42-43)

No.(s) _____;

M.M. ♩ = _____;

key(s): E♭ a e E

Articulation:

legato   staccato   portato

Dynamic:

f   p   mf   mp   ff   pp

Dynamic Variant

left hand *f* — right hand *p*

Articulation Variant

left hand *staccato* — right hand *legato*

Rhythmic Variant

B. Prepared Sightreading Piece

Play at least three times each week. Keep a steady beat.

For directions, see *How to Use This Book* on page 50.

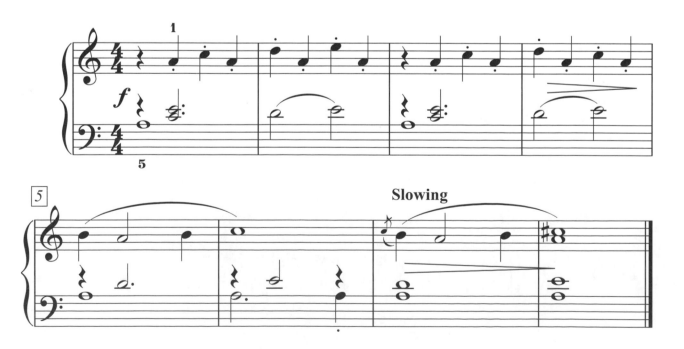

C. Aural Skills - Rhythmic   For directions, see *How to Use This Book* on page 50.

Tap each exercise with the backing track to *Rockin' in the Aisles* while counting out loud.
- start with the Practice track, progress to the Performance track
- count an ♪ pulse "1 - & - 2 - & - 3 - & - 4 - &"

out loud as you tap:
- i) First tap the lower rhythm on your left thigh.
- ii) Then tap the top rhythm on your right thigh.
- iii) Finally tap both rhythms, hands together.

a)

b)

c)

D. Aural Skills - Pitch   For directions, see *How to Use This Book* on page 50.

1) a) Play the ♩ part at the piano while singing the ♩ part. Identify each interval: size – 1, 2, 3, 4, or 5; and quality – M (major), m (minor), or P (perfect).

b) Play the cadence. Then sing the top part while playing the bass line.

2) Sing and play the phrase simultaneously. Repeat, but don't play the last two bars – just sing them. Finally, just sing the entire phrase.

Unit Three - Module One

A. Technic

Set weekly practice schedule as assigned by your teacher. For directions, see *How to Use This Book* on page 50.

1) Chords (pages 44-45)

No.(s) _____;

M.M. ♩ = _____;

key(s): e E g d

2) Arpeggios (page 46)

No.(s) _____;

M.M. ♩ = _____;

key(s): E g c

3) Blues Scales (page 47)

No.(s) _____;

M.M. ♩ = _____;

key(s): D A F

4) Drills (pages 48-49)

No.(s) _____;

M.M. ♩ = _____;

key(s): F♯ C♯

5) Scales (pages 42-43)

No.(s) _____;

M.M. ♩ = ___ · ___;

key(s): e E g d

Articulation:

    legato   *staccato*   *portato*

Dynamic:

  f   *p*   *mf*   *mp*   *ff*   *pp*

Dynamic Variant

< to top, > to bottom

Articulation Variant

  left hand *staccato* — right hand *legato*

Rhythmic Variant

B. Prepared Sightreading Piece

Play at least three times each week. Keep a steady beat.

For directions, see *How to Use This Book* on page 50.

C. Aural Skills - Rhythmic   For directions, see *How to Use This Book* on page 50.

Tap each exercise with the backing track to *Ready for Action* while counting out loud.
- start with the Practice track, progress to the Performance track
- count an ♪ pulse "1 - & - 2 - & - 3 - & - 4 - &"

out loud as you tap:
- i)   First tap the lower rhythm on your left thigh.
- ii) Then tap the top rhythm on your right thigh.
- iii) Finally tap both rhythms, hands together.

a)

b)

c)

D. Aural Skills - Pitch   For directions, see *How to Use This Book* on page 50.

1) a) Play the ♩ part at the piano while singing the ♩ part. Identify each interval: size – 1, 2, 3, 4, or 5; and quality – M (major), m (minor), or P (perfect).

b) Play the cadence. Then sing the top part while playing the bass line.

2) Sing and play the phrase simultaneously. Repeat, but don't play the last two bars – just sing them. Finally, just sing the entire phrase.

Unit Three - Module Two

A. Technic

Set weekly practice schedule as assigned by your teacher. For directions, see *How to Use This Book* on page 50.

1) Chords (pages 44-45)

No.(s) _____ ;

M.M. ♩ = _____ ;

key(s): e E g d

2) Arpeggios (page 46)

No.(s) _____ ;

M.M. ♩ = _____ ;

key(s): E g c

3) Blues Scales (page 47)

No.(s) _____ ;

M.M. ♩ = _____ ;

key(s): D A F

4) Drills (pages 48-49)

No.(s) _____ ;

M.M. ♩ = _____ ;

key(s): F♯ C♯

5) Scales (pages 42-43)

No.(s) _____ ;

M.M. ♩ = _____ ;

key(s): e E g d

Articulation:

    legato   *staccato*   *portato*

Dynamic:

    f   *p*   *mf*   *mp*   *ff*   *pp*

> **Dynamic Variant**
>
> > to top,   < to bottom
>
> **Articulation Variant**
>
> left hand *staccato* — right hand *legato*
>
> **Rhythmic Variant**

B. Prepared Sightreading Piece

Play at least three times each week. Keep a steady beat.

For directions, see *How to Use This Book* on page 50.

C. Aural Skills - Rhythmic   For directions, see *How to Use This Book* on page 50.

Tap each exercise with the backing track to *Trucking Along* while counting out loud.
- start with the Practice track, progress to the Performance track
- count a swung ♪ pulse "1 - a - 2 - a - 3 - a - 4 - a"

out loud as you tap:
i) First tap the lower rhythm on your left thigh.
ii) Then tap the top rhythm on your right thigh.
iii) Finally tap both rhythms, hands together.

a)

b)

c)

D. Aural Skills - Pitch   For directions, see *How to Use This Book* on page 50.

1) a) Play the ♩ part at the piano while singing the ♩ part. Identify each interval: size – 1, 2, 3, 4, or 5; and quality – M (major), m (minor), or P (perfect).

b) Play the cadence. Then sing the top part while playing the bass line.

2) Sing and play the phrase simultaneously. Repeat, but don't play the last two bars – just sing them. Finally, just sing the entire phrase.

Unit Three - Module Three

A. Technic

Set weekly practice schedule as assigned by your teacher. For directions, see *How to Use This Book* on page 50.

1) Chords (pages 44-45)

No.(s) _____ ;

M.M. ♩ = _____ ;

key(s): e E g d

2) Arpeggios (page 46)

No.(s) _____ ;

M.M. ♩ = _____ ;

key(s): E g c

3) Blues Scales (page 47)

No.(s) _____ ;

M.M. ♩ = _____ ;

key(s): D A F

4) Drills (pages 48-49)

No.(s) _____ ;

M.M. ♩ = _____ ;

key(s): F♯ C♯

5) Scales (pages 42-43)

No.(s) _____ ;

M.M. ♩ = _____ ;

key(s): e E g d

Articulation:

legato   *staccato*   *portato*

Dynamic:

f   *p*   *mf*   *mp*   *ff*   *pp*

> **Dynamic Variant**
>
> left hand ***p*** — right hand ***f***
>
> **Articulation Variant**
>
> left hand *staccato* — right hand *legato*
>
> **Rhythmic Variant**

B. Prepared Sightreading Piece

Play at least three times each week. Keep a steady beat.

For directions, see *How to Use This Book* on page 50.

C. Aural Skills - Rhythmic
For directions, see *How to Use This Book* on page 50.

Tap each exercise with the backing track to *Rockin' in the Aisles* while counting out loud.
- start with the Practice track, progress to the Performance track
- count an ♪ pulse "1 - & - 2 - & - 3 - & - 4 - &"

out loud as you tap:
- i)   First tap the lower rhythm on your left thigh.
- ii) Then tap the top rhythm on your right thigh.
- iii) Finally tap both rhythms, hands together.

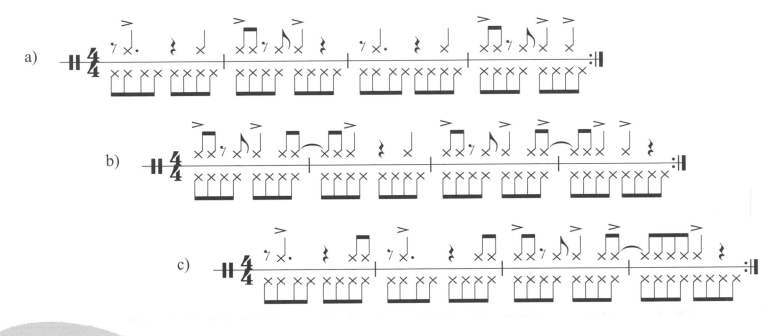

a)

b)

c)

D. Aural Skills - Pitch
For directions, see *How to Use This Book* on page 50.

1) a) Play the 𝅗𝅥 part at the piano while singing the ♩ part. Identify each interval: size – 1, 2, 3, 4, or 5; and quality – M (major), m (minor), or P (perfect).

b) Play the cadence. Then sing the top part while playing the bass line.

2) Sing and play the phrase simultaneously. Repeat, but don't play the last two bars – just sing them. Finally, just sing the entire phrase.

Unit Three - Module Four

A. Technic

Set weekly practice schedule as assigned by your teacher. For directions, see *How to Use This Book* on page 50.

1) Chords (pages 44-45)

No.(s) _____;

M.M. ♩ = _____;

key(s): e E g d

2) Arpeggios (page 46)

No.(s) _____;

M.M. ♩ = _____;

key(s): E g c

3) Blues Scales (page 47)

No.(s) _____;

M.M. ♩ = _____;

key(s): D A F

4) Drills (pages 48-49)

No.(s) _____;

M.M. ♩ = _____;

key(s): F♯ C♯

5) Scales (pages 42-43)

No.(s) _____;

M.M. ♩ = _____;

key(s): e E g d

Articulation:

  legato *staccato* *portato*

Dynamic:

  f *p* *mf* *mp* *ff* *pp*

Dynamic Variant

  left hand *f* — right hand *p*

Articulation Variant

  left hand *staccato* — right hand *legato*

Rhythmic Variant

B. Prepared Sightreading Piece

Play at least three times each week. Keep a steady beat.

For directions, see *How to Use This Book* on page 50.

C. Aural Skills - Rhythmic   For directions, see *How to Use This Book* on page 50.

Tap each exercise with the backing track to *Waltz of Regret* while counting out loud.
- start with the Practice track, progress to the Performance track
- count an ♪ pulse "1 - & - 2 - & - 3 - &" out

loud as you tap:
  i)   First tap the lower rhythm on your left thigh.
  ii) Then tap the top rhythm on your right thigh.
  iii) Finally tap both rhythms, hands together.

a)

b)

c)

D. Aural Skills - Pitch   For directions, see *How to Use This Book* on page 50.

1) a) Play the ♩ part at the piano while singing the ♩ part. Identify each interval: size – 1, 2, 3, 4, or 5; and quality – M (major), m (minor), or P (perfect).

b) Play the cadence. Then sing the top part while playing the bass line.

2) Sing and play the phrase simultaneously. Repeat, but don't play the last two bars – just sing them. Finally, just sing the entire phrase.

Unit Four - Module One

A. Technic

Set weekly practice schedule as assigned by your teacher. For directions, see *How to Use This Book* on page 50.

1) Chords (pages 44-45)

No.(s) _____ ;

M.M. ♩ = _____ ;

key(s): g   d   A♭   f

2) Arpeggios (page 46)

No.(s) _____ ;

M.M. ♩ = _____ ;

key(s): g   c   f

3) Blues Scales (page 47)

No.(s) _____ ;

M.M. ♩ = _____ ;

key(s): A   F   B♭

4) Drills (pages 48-49)

No.(s) _____ ;

M.M. ♩ = _____ ;

key(s): f♯   c♯

5) Scales (pages 42-43)

No.(s) _____ ;

M.M. ♩ = _____ ;

key(s): g   d   A♭   f

Articulation:

   legato   staccato   portato

Dynamic:

   f   p   mf   mp   ff   pp

Dynamic Variant

< to top,   > to bottom

Articulation Variant

left hand *legato* — right hand *staccato*

Rhythmic Variant

B. Prepared Sightreading Piece

Play at least three times each week. Keep a steady beat.

For directions, see *How to Use This Book* on page 50.

C. Aural Skills - Rhythmic
For directions, see *How to Use This Book* on page 50.

Tap each exercise with the backing track to *Trucking Along* while counting out loud.
- start with the Practice track, progress to the Performance track
- count a swung ♪ pulse "1 - a - 2 - a - 3 - a - 4 - a"

out loud as you tap:
- i) First tap the lower rhythm on your left thigh.
- ii) Then tap the top rhythm on your right thigh.
- iii) Finally tap both rhythms, hands together.

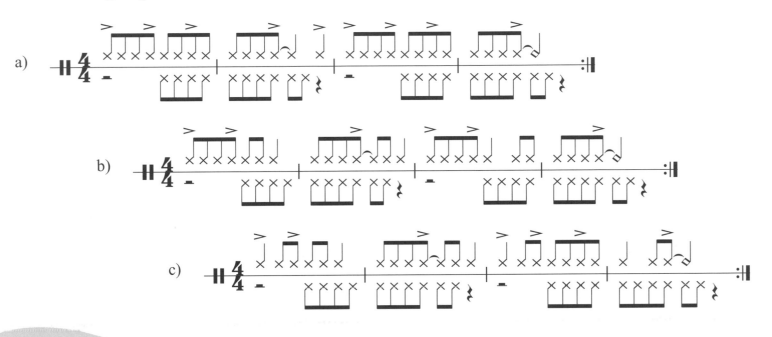

D. Aural Skills - Pitch
For directions, see *How to Use This Book* on page 50.

1) a) Play the ♩ part at the piano while singing the ♩ part. Identify each interval: size – 1, 2, 3, 4, or 5; and quality – M (major), m (minor), or P (perfect).

b) Play the cadence. Then sing the top part while playing the bass line.

2) Sing and play the phrase simultaneously. Repeat, but don't play the last two bars – just sing them. Finally, just sing the entire phrase.

Unit Four - Module Two

A. Technic

Set weekly practice schedule as assigned by your teacher. For directions, see *How to Use This Book* on page 50.

1) Chords (pages 44-45)

No.(s) _____ ;

M.M. ♩ = _____ ;

key(s): g   d   A♭   f

2) Arpeggios (page 46)

No.(s) _____ ;

M.M. _____ ♩ = _____ ;

key(s): g   c   f

3) Blues Scales (page 47)

No.(s) _____ ;

M.M. ♩ = _____ ;

key(s): A   F   B♭

4) Drills (pages 48-49)

No.(s) _____ ;

M.M. ♩ = _____ ;

key(s): f♯   c♯

5) Scales (pages 42-43)

No.(s) _____ ;

M.M. ♩ = _____ ;

key(s): g   d   A♭   f

Articulation:

    legato   *staccato*   *portato*

Dynamic:

    f   *p*   *mf*   *mp*   *ff*   *pp*

Dynamic Variant

> to top, < to bottom

Articulation Variant

left hand *legato* — right hand *staccato*

Rhythmic Variant

B. Prepared Sightreading Piece

Play at least three times each week. Keep a steady beat.

For directions, see *How to Use This Book* on page 50.

C. Aural Skills - Rhythmic

For directions, see *How to Use This Book* on page 50.

Tap each exercise with the backing track to *Rockin' in the Aisles* while counting out loud.
- start with the Practice track, progress to the Performance track
- count an ♪ pulse "1 - & - 2 - & - 3 - & - 4 - &"

out loud as you tap:
  i) First tap the lower rhythm on your left thigh.
  ii) Then tap the top rhythm on your right thigh.
  iii) Finally tap both rhythms, hands together.

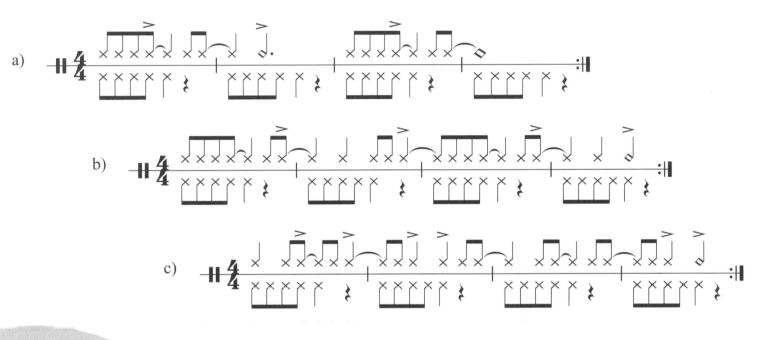

D. Aural Skills - Pitch

For directions, see *How to Use This Book* on page 50.

1) a) Play the 𝅗𝅥 part at the piano while singing the ♩ part. Identify each interval: size – 1, 2, 3, 4, or 5; and quality – M (major), m (minor), or P (perfect).

b) Play the cadence. Then sing the top part while playing the bass line.

2) Sing and play the phrase simultaneously. Repeat, but don't play the last two bars – just sing them. Finally, just sing the entire phrase.

Unit Four - Module Three

A. Technic

Set weekly practice schedule as assigned by your teacher. For directions, see *How to Use This Book* on page 50.

1) Chords (pages 44-45)

No.(s) _____ ;

M.M. ♩ = _____ ;

key(s): g   d   A♭   f

2) Arpeggios (page 46)

No.(s) _____ ;

M.M. ♩ = _____ ;

key(s): g   c   f

3) Blues Scales (page 47)

No.(s) _____ ;

M.M. ♩ = _____ ;

key(s): A   F   B♭

4) Drills (pages 48-49)

No.(s) _____ ;

M.M. ♩ = _____ ;

key(s): f♯   c♯

5) Scales (pages 42-43)

No.(s) _____ ;

M.M. ♩ = _____ ;

key(s): g   d   A♭   f

Articulation:

legato   *staccato*   *portato*

Dynamic:

𝆑   𝆏   𝑚𝑓   𝑚𝑝   𝆑𝆑   𝆏𝆏

Dynamic Variant

left hand 𝒑 — right hand 𝒇

Articulation Variant

left hand *legato* — right hand *staccato*

Rhythmic Variant

B. Prepared Sightreading Piece

Play at least three times each week. Keep a steady beat.

For directions, see *How to Use This Book* on page 50.

C. Aural Skills - Rhythmic   For directions, see *How to Use This Book* on page 50.

Tap each exercise with the backing track to *Waltz of Regret* while counting out loud.
- start with the Practice track, progress to the Performance track
- count an ♪ pulse "1 - & - 2 - & - 3 - &" out loud as you tap:

i) First tap the lower rhythm on your left thigh.
ii) Then tap the top rhythm on your right thigh.
iii) Finally tap both rhythms, hands together.

a)

b)

c)

D. Aural Skills - Pitch   For directions, see *How to Use This Book* on page 50.

1) a) Play the ♩ part at the piano while singing the ♩ part. Identify each interval: size – 1, 2, 3, 4, or 5; and quality – M (major), m (minor), or P (perfect).

b) Play the cadence. Then sing the top part while playing the bass line.

2) Sing and play the phrase simultaneously. Repeat, but don't play the last two bars – just sing them. Finally, just sing the entire phrase.

Unit Four - Module Four

A. Technic

Set weekly practice schedule as assigned by your teacher. For directions, see *How to Use This Book* on page 50.

1) Chords (pages 44-45)

No.(s) _____ ;

M.M. ♩ = _____ ;

key(s): g   d   A♭   f

2) Arpeggios (page 46)

No.(s) _____ ;

M.M. ♩ = _____ ;

key(s): g   c   f

3) Blues Scales (page 47)

No.(s) _____ ;

M.M. ♩ = _____ ;

key(s): A   F   B♭

4) Drills (pages 48-49)

No.(s) _____ ;

M.M. ♩ = _____ ;

key(s): f♯   c♯

5) Scales (pages 42-43)

No.(s) _____ ;

M.M. ♩ = _____ ;

key(s): g   d   A♭   f

Articulation:

legato   staccato   portato

Dynamic:

𝆑   𝆏   𝐦𝐟   𝐦𝐩   𝆑𝆑   𝆏𝆏

Dynamic Variant

left hand 𝆑 — right hand 𝆏

Articulation Variant

left hand *legato* — right hand *staccato*

Rhythmic Variant

B. Prepared Sightreading Piece

Play at least three times each week. Keep a steady beat.

For directions, see *How to Use This Book* on page 50.

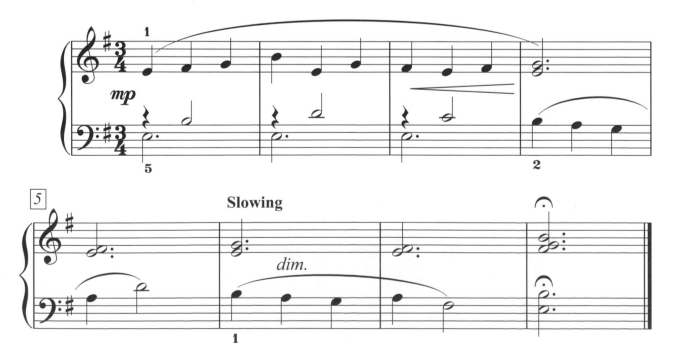

C. Aural Skills - Rhythmic   For directions, see *How to Use This Book* on page 50.

Tap each exercise with the backing track to *Ready for Action* while counting out loud.
- start with the Practice track, progress to the Performance track
- count an ♪ pulse "1 - & - 2 - & - 3 - & - 4 - &"

out loud as you tap:
- i)   First tap the lower rhythm on your left thigh.
- ii) Then tap the top rhythm on your right thigh.
- iii) Finally tap both rhythms, hands together.

a)

b)

c)

D. Aural Skills - Pitch   For directions, see *How to Use This Book* on page 50.

1) a) Play the ♩ part at the piano while singing the ♩ part. Identify each interval: size – 1, 2, 3, 4, or 5; and quality – M (major), m (minor), or P (perfect).

b) Play the cadence. Then sing the top part while playing the bass line.

2) Sing and play the phrase simultaneously. Repeat, but don't play the last two bars – just sing them. Finally, just sing the entire phrase.

Unit 1 - Midterm

I. Technic   Grade [ ]

A. Chords
No.(s) _____ ; key(s) _____ ; M.M. _____ ;

B. Arpeggios
No.(s) _____ ; key(s) _____ ; M.M. _____ ;

C. Blues Scales
No.(s) _____ ; key(s) _____ ; M.M. _____ ;

D. Drills
No.(s) _____ ; key(s) _____ ; M.M. _____ ;

E. Scales
No.(s) _____ ; key(s) _____ ; M.M. _____ ;

II. Sightreading   Grade [ ]   Student may study for up to 15 seconds.

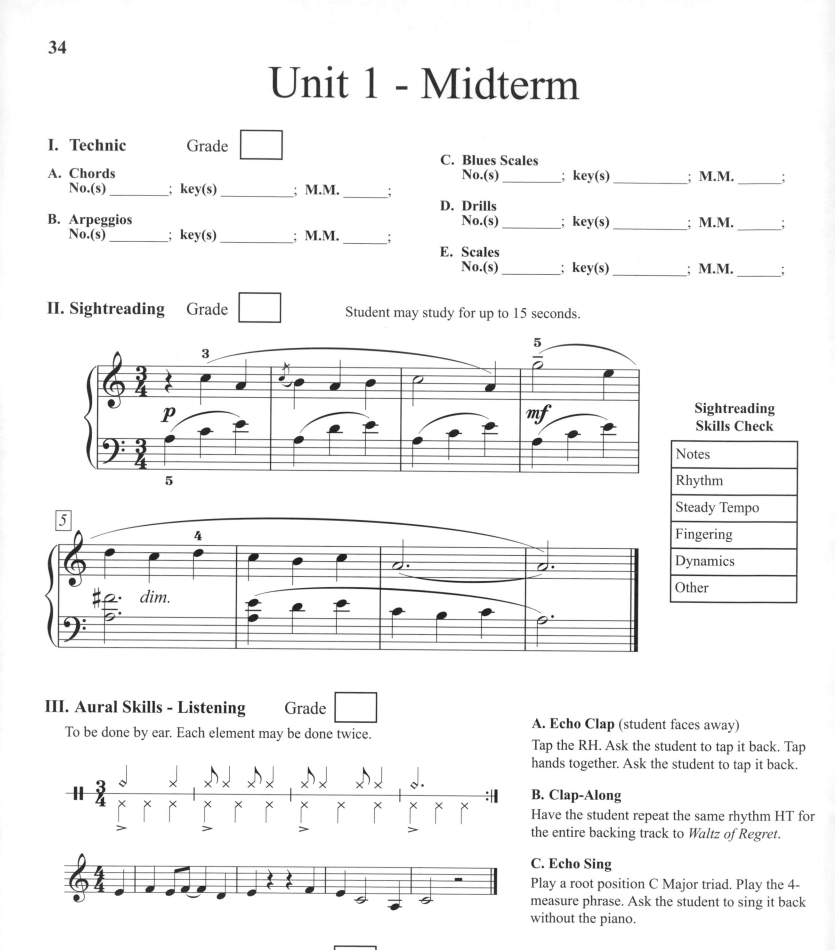

Sightreading Skills Check

| Notes |
| Rhythm |
| Steady Tempo |
| Fingering |
| Dynamics |
| Other |

III. Aural Skills - Listening   Grade [ ]

To be done by ear. Each element may be done twice.

A. Echo Clap (student faces away)

Tap the RH. Ask the student to tap it back. Tap hands together. Ask the student to tap it back.

B. Clap-Along

Have the student repeat the same rhythm HT for the entire backing track to *Waltz of Regret*.

C. Echo Sing

Play a root position C Major triad. Play the 4-measure phrase. Ask the student to sing it back without the piano.

IV. Aural Skills - Reading   Grade [ ]

To be done at sight. Each element may be done twice.

A. Interval Sing (student looks at music)
1. Play a root position d minor triad.
2. Ask the student to sing the ♩ part as you play both the ♩ and ♪ parts.
3. Repeat, playing only the ♩ part as the student sings the ♪ part.

Unit 1 - Final

I. Technic   Grade [   ]

A. Chords
No.(s) _____ ; key(s) _____ ; M.M. _____ ;

B. Arpeggios
No.(s) _____ ; key(s) _____ ; M.M. _____ ;

C. Blues Scales
No.(s) _____ ; key(s) _____ ; M.M. _____ ;

D. Drills
No.(s) _____ ; key(s) _____ ; M.M. _____ ;

E. Scales
No.(s) _____ ; key(s) _____ ; M.M. _____ ;

II. Sightreading   Grade [   ]   Student may study for up to 15 seconds.

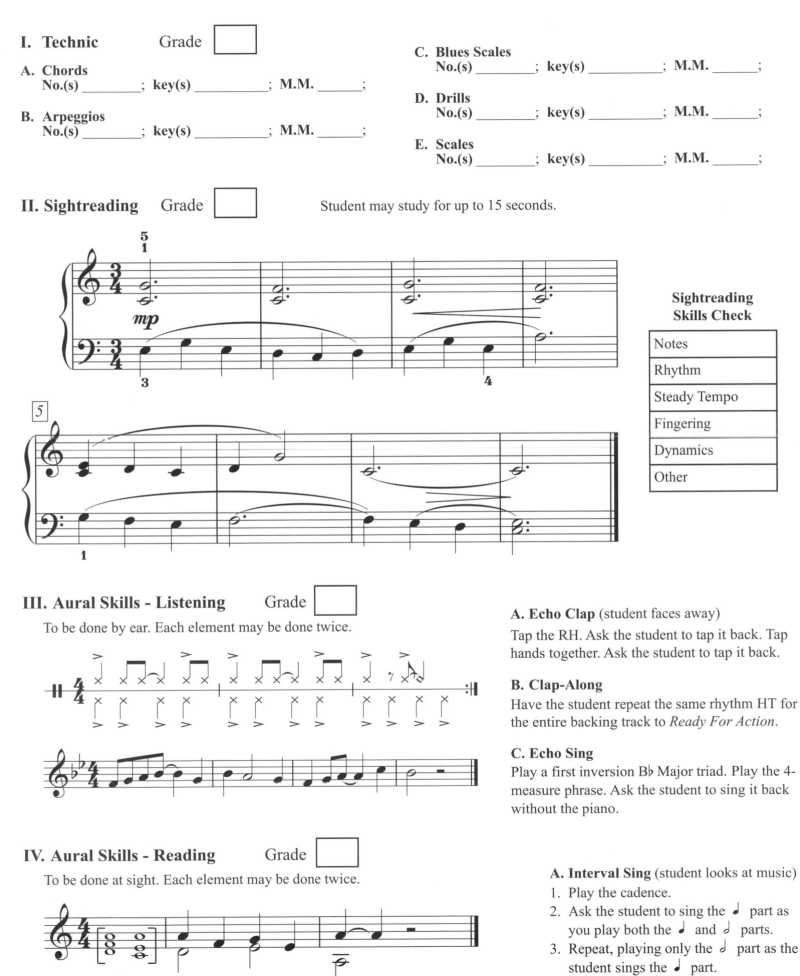

Sightreading Skills Check

Notes
Rhythm
Steady Tempo
Fingering
Dynamics
Other

III. Aural Skills - Listening   Grade [   ]

To be done by ear. Each element may be done twice.

A. Echo Clap (student faces away)

Tap the RH. Ask the student to tap it back. Tap hands together. Ask the student to tap it back.

B. Clap-Along

Have the student repeat the same rhythm HT for the entire backing track to *Ready For Action*.

C. Echo Sing

Play a first inversion B♭ Major triad. Play the 4-measure phrase. Ask the student to sing it back without the piano.

IV. Aural Skills - Reading   Grade [   ]

To be done at sight. Each element may be done twice.

A. Interval Sing (student looks at music)
1. Play the cadence.
2. Ask the student to sing the ♩ part as you play both the ♩ and ♪ parts.
3. Repeat, playing only the ♪ part as the student sings the ♩ part.

Unit 2 - Midterm

I. Technic Grade ☐

A. Chords
No.(s) _____ ; key(s) _____ ; M.M. _____ ;

B. Arpeggios
No.(s) _____ ; key(s) _____ ; M.M. _____ ;

C. Blues Scales
No.(s) _____ ; key(s) _____ ; M.M. _____ ;

D. Drills
No.(s) _____ ; key(s) _____ ; M.M. _____ ;

E. Scales
No.(s) _____ ; key(s) _____ ; M.M. _____ ;

II. Sightreading Grade ☐   Student may study for up to 15 seconds.

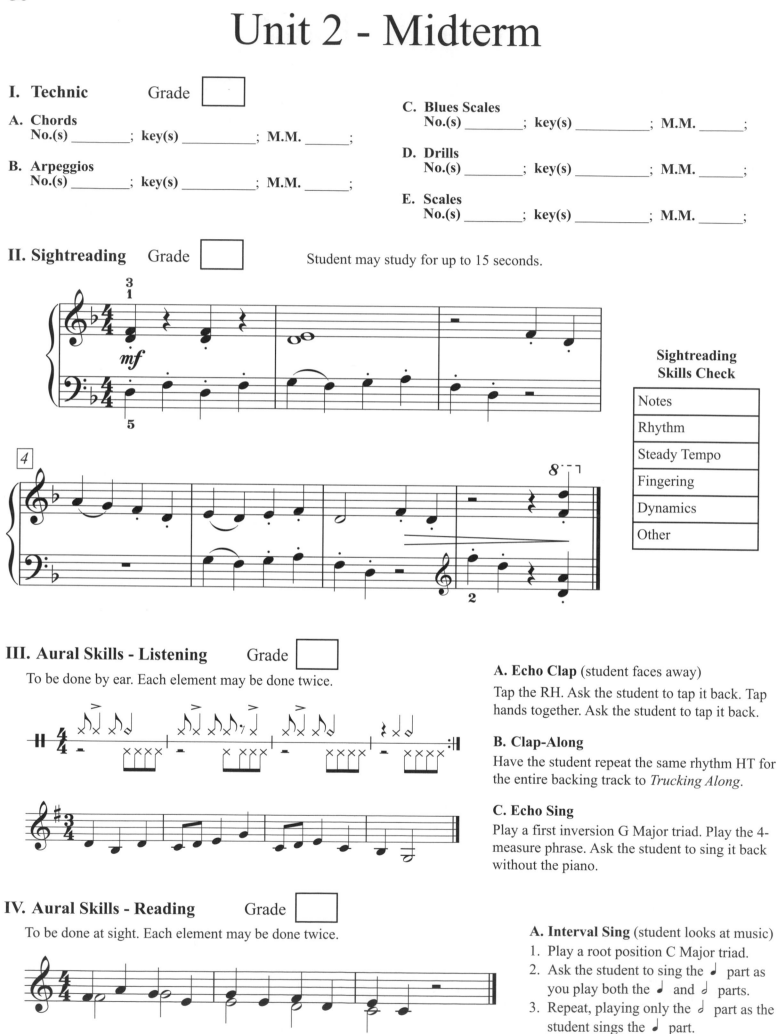

Sightreading Skills Check

| Notes |
| Rhythm |
| Steady Tempo |
| Fingering |
| Dynamics |
| Other |

III. Aural Skills - Listening Grade ☐

To be done by ear. Each element may be done twice.

A. Echo Clap (student faces away)
Tap the RH. Ask the student to tap it back. Tap hands together. Ask the student to tap it back.

B. Clap-Along
Have the student repeat the same rhythm HT for the entire backing track to *Trucking Along*.

C. Echo Sing
Play a first inversion G Major triad. Play the 4-measure phrase. Ask the student to sing it back without the piano.

IV. Aural Skills - Reading Grade ☐

To be done at sight. Each element may be done twice.

A. Interval Sing (student looks at music)
1. Play a root position C Major triad.
2. Ask the student to sing the ♩ part as you play both the ♩ and ♩ parts.
3. Repeat, playing only the ♩ part as the student sings the ♩ part.

Unit 2 - Final

I. Technic   Grade ☐

A. Chords
No.(s) _____ ; key(s) _____ ; M.M. _____ ;

B. Arpeggios
No.(s) _____ ; key(s) _____ ; M.M. _____ ;

C. Blues Scales
No.(s) _____ ; key(s) _____ ; M.M. _____ ;

D. Drills
No.(s) _____ ; key(s) _____ ; M.M. _____ ;

E. Scales
No.(s) _____ ; key(s) _____ ; M.M. _____ ;

II. Sightreading   Grade ☐   Student may study for up to 15 seconds.

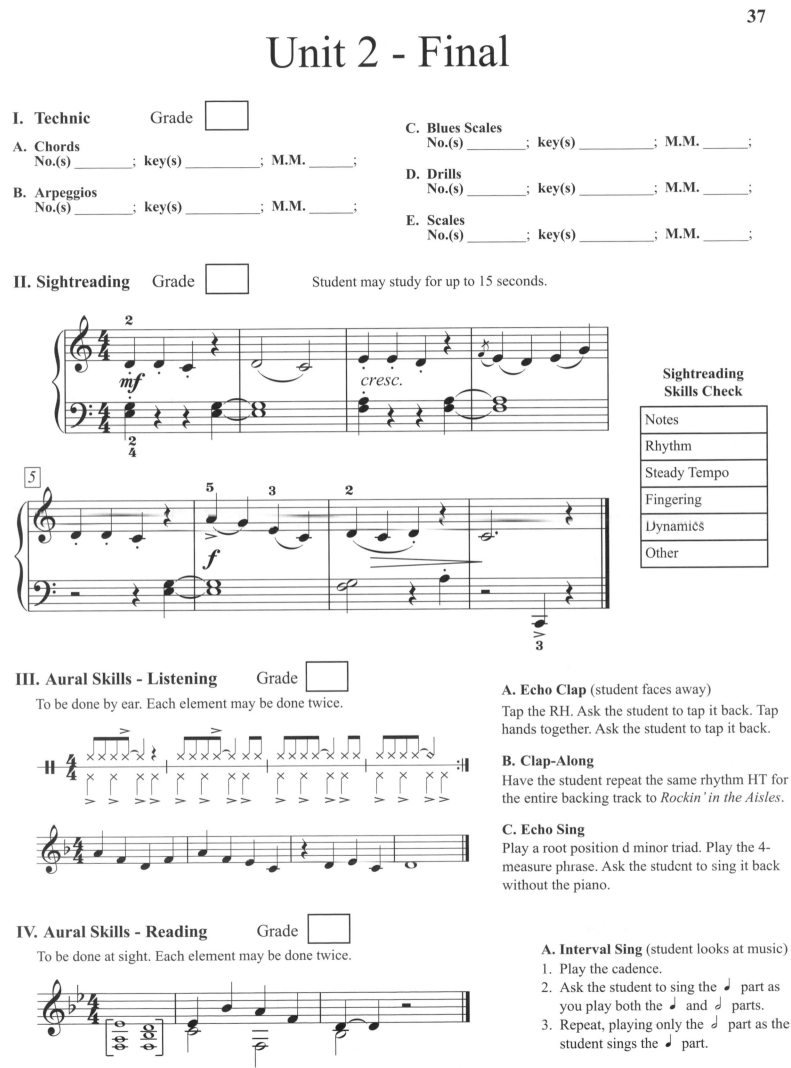

Sightreading Skills Check
Notes
Rhythm
Steady Tempo
Fingering
Dynamics
Other

III. Aural Skills - Listening   Grade ☐

To be done by ear. Each element may be done twice.

A. Echo Clap (student faces away)

Tap the RH. Ask the student to tap it back. Tap hands together. Ask the student to tap it back.

B. Clap-Along

Have the student repeat the same rhythm HT for the entire backing track to *Rockin' in the Aisles*.

C. Echo Sing

Play a root position d minor triad. Play the 4-measure phrase. Ask the student to sing it back without the piano.

IV. Aural Skills - Reading   Grade ☐

To be done at sight. Each element may be done twice.

A. Interval Sing (student looks at music)

1. Play the cadence.
2. Ask the student to sing the ♩ part as you play both the ♩ and ♪ parts.
3. Repeat, playing only the ♪ part as the student sings the ♩ part.

Unit 3 - Midterm

I. Technic Grade ☐

A. Chords
No.(s) _____ ; key(s) _____ ; M.M. _____ ;

B. Arpeggios
No.(s) _____ ; key(s) _____ ; M.M. _____ ;

C. Blues Scales
No.(s) _____ ; key(s) _____ ; M.M. _____ ;

D. Drills
No.(s) _____ ; key(s) _____ ; M.M. _____ ;

E. Scales
No.(s) _____ ; key(s) _____ ; M.M. _____ ;

II. Sightreading Grade ☐   Student may study for up to 15 seconds.

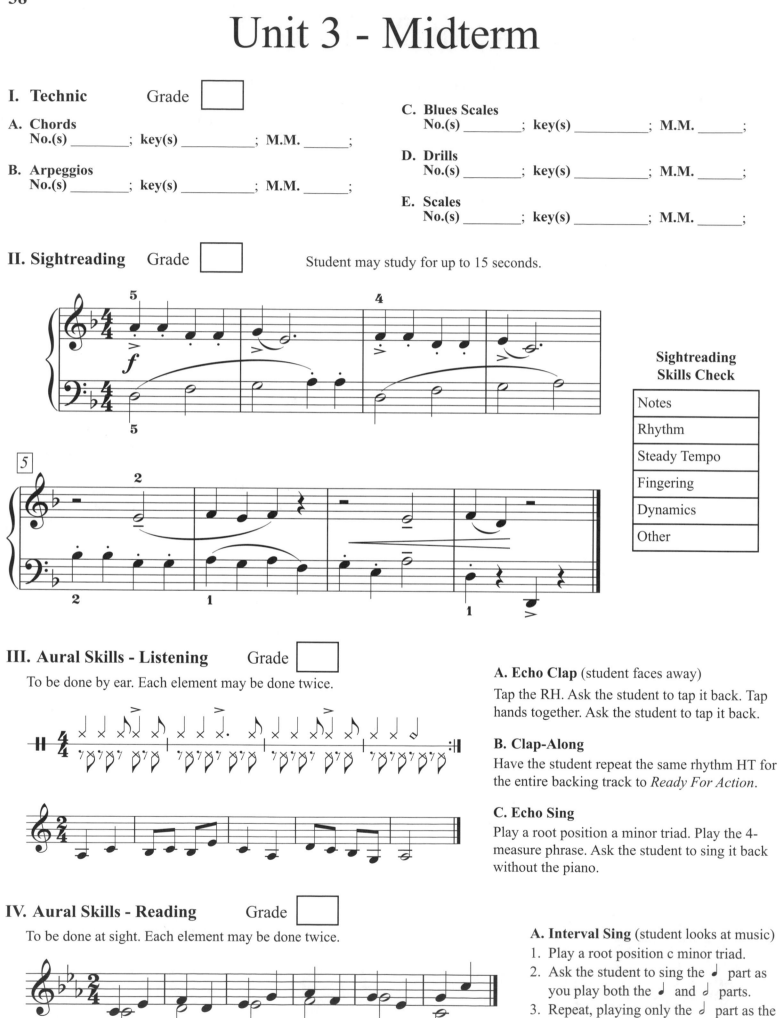

Sightreading Skills Check
Notes
Rhythm
Steady Tempo
Fingering
Dynamics
Other

III. Aural Skills - Listening Grade ☐

To be done by ear. Each element may be done twice.

A. Echo Clap (student faces away)

Tap the RH. Ask the student to tap it back. Tap hands together. Ask the student to tap it back.

B. Clap-Along

Have the student repeat the same rhythm HT for the entire backing track to *Ready For Action*.

C. Echo Sing

Play a root position a minor triad. Play the 4-measure phrase. Ask the student to sing it back without the piano.

IV. Aural Skills - Reading Grade ☐

To be done at sight. Each element may be done twice.

A. Interval Sing (student looks at music)

1. Play a root position c minor triad.
2. Ask the student to sing the ♩ part as you play both the ♩ and ♪ parts.
3. Repeat, playing only the ♩ part as the student sings the ♩ part.

Unit 3 - Final

I. Technic   Grade ☐

A. Chords
No.(s) _____ ; key(s) _____ ; M.M. _____ ;

B. Arpeggios
No.(s) _____ ; key(s) _____ ; M.M. _____ ;

C. Blues Scales
No.(s) _____ ; key(s) _____ ; M.M. _____ ;

D. Drills
No.(s) _____ ; key(s) _____ ; M.M. _____ ;

E. Scales
No.(s) _____ ; key(s) _____ ; M.M. _____ ;

II. Sightreading   Grade ☐   Student may study for up to 15 seconds.

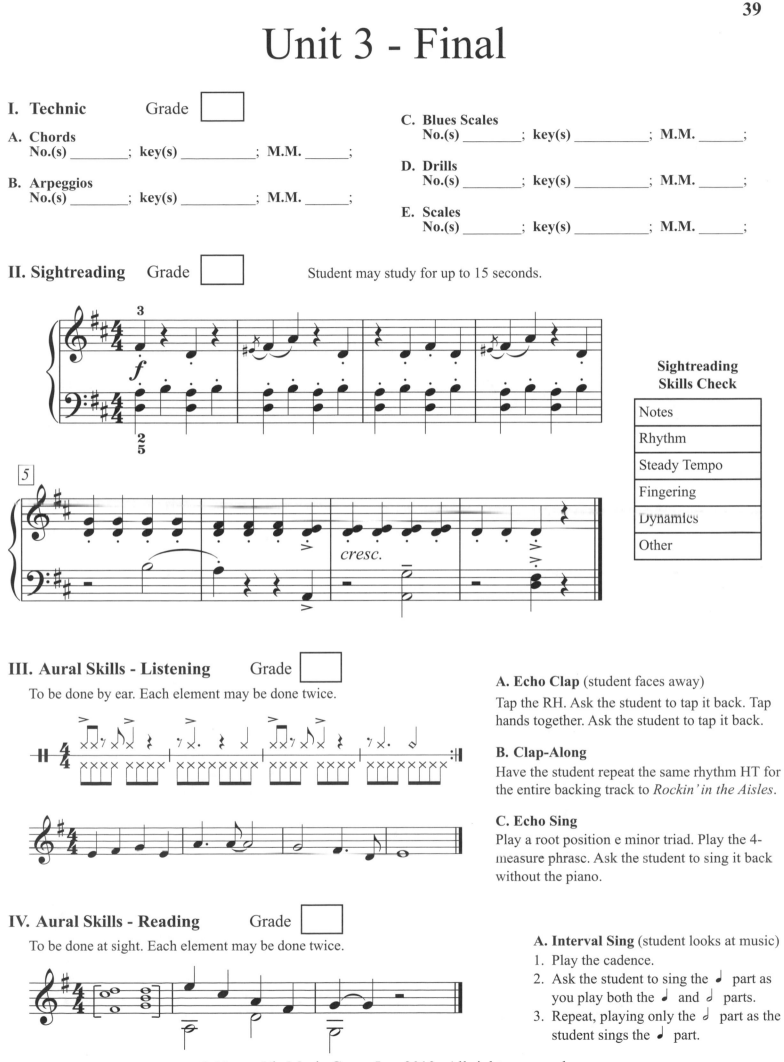

Sightreading Skills Check
Notes
Rhythm
Steady Tempo
Fingering
Dynamics
Other

III. Aural Skills - Listening   Grade ☐

To be done by ear. Each element may be done twice.

A. Echo Clap (student faces away)
Tap the RH. Ask the student to tap it back. Tap hands together. Ask the student to tap it back.

B. Clap-Along
Have the student repeat the same rhythm HT for the entire backing track to *Rockin' in the Aisles.*

C. Echo Sing
Play a root position e minor triad. Play the 4-measure phrase. Ask the student to sing it back without the piano.

IV. Aural Skills - Reading   Grade ☐

To be done at sight. Each element may be done twice.

A. Interval Sing (student looks at music)
1. Play the cadence.
2. Ask the student to sing the ♩ part as you play both the ♩ and ♪ parts.
3. Repeat, playing only the ♪ part as the student sings the ♩ part.

Unit 4 - Midterm

I. Technic   Grade ☐

A. Chords
No.(s) _____ ; key(s) _____ ; M.M. _____ ;

B. Arpeggios
No.(s) _____ ; key(s) _____ ; M.M. _____ ;

C. Blues Scales
No.(s) _____ ; key(s) _____ ; M.M. _____ ;

D. Drills
No.(s) _____ ; key(s) _____ ; M.M. _____ ;

E. Scales
No.(s) _____ ; key(s) _____ ; M.M. _____ ;

II. Sightreading   Grade ☐   Student may study for up to 15 seconds.

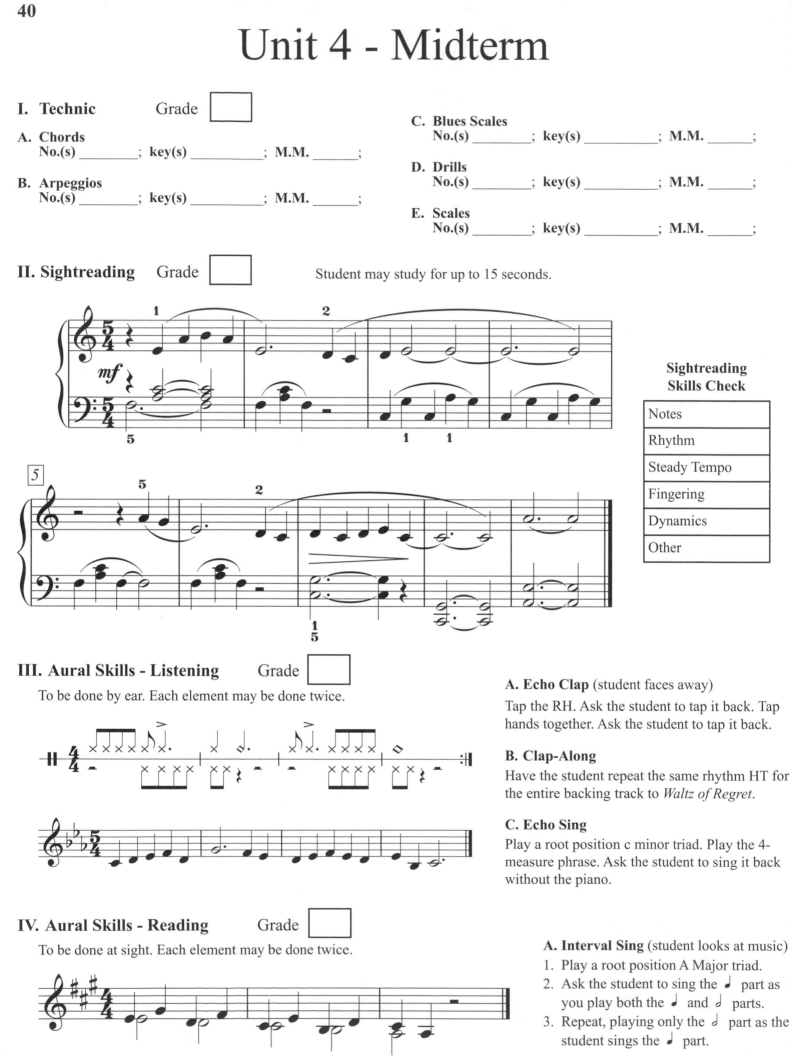

Sightreading Skills Check

| Notes |
| Rhythm |
| Steady Tempo |
| Fingering |
| Dynamics |
| Other |

III. Aural Skills - Listening   Grade ☐

To be done by ear. Each element may be done twice.

A. Echo Clap (student faces away)

Tap the RH. Ask the student to tap it back. Tap hands together. Ask the student to tap it back.

B. Clap-Along

Have the student repeat the same rhythm HT for the entire backing track to *Waltz of Regret*.

C. Echo Sing

Play a root position c minor triad. Play the 4-measure phrase. Ask the student to sing it back without the piano.

IV. Aural Skills - Reading   Grade ☐

To be done at sight. Each element may be done twice.

A. Interval Sing (student looks at music)
1. Play a root position A Major triad.
2. Ask the student to sing the ♩ part as you play both the ♩ and 𝅗𝅥 parts.
3. Repeat, playing only the 𝅗𝅥 part as the student sings the ♩ part.

Unit 4 - Final

I. Technic   Grade ☐

A. Chords
No.(s) _____ ; key(s) _____ ; M.M. _____ ;

B. Arpeggios
No.(s) _____ ; key(s) _____ ; M.M. _____ ;

C. Blues Scales
No.(s) _____ ; key(s) _____ ; M.M. _____ ;

D. Drills
No.(s) _____ ; key(s) _____ ; M.M. _____ ;

E. Scales
No.(s) _____ ; key(s) _____ ; M.M. _____ ;

II. Sightreading   Grade ☐   Student may study for up to 15 seconds.

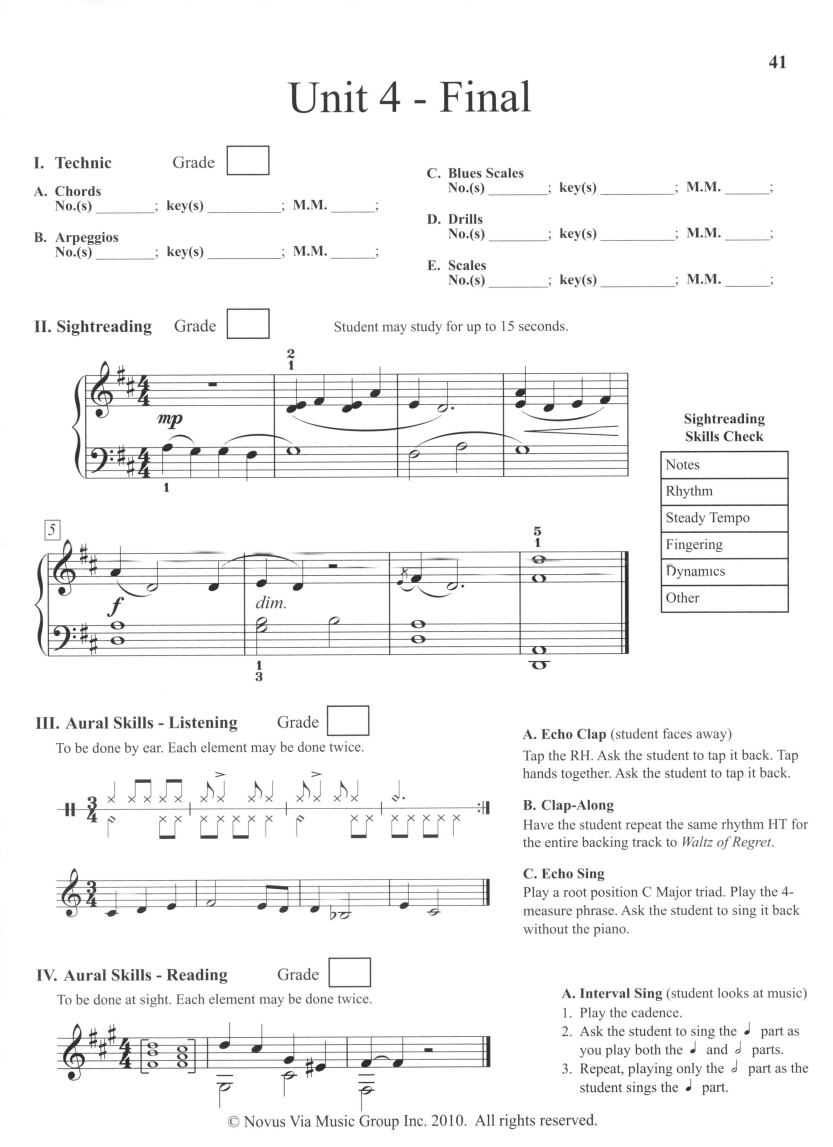

Sightreading Skills Check	
Notes	
Rhythm	
Steady Tempo	
Fingering	
Dynamics	
Other	

III. Aural Skills - Listening   Grade ☐

To be done by ear. Each element may be done twice.

A. Echo Clap (student faces away)
Tap the RH. Ask the student to tap it back. Tap hands together. Ask the student to tap it back.

B. Clap-Along
Have the student repeat the same rhythm HT for the entire backing track to *Waltz of Regret*.

C. Echo Sing
Play a root position C Major triad. Play the 4-measure phrase. Ask the student to sing it back without the piano.

IV. Aural Skills - Reading   Grade ☐

To be done at sight. Each element may be done twice.

A. Interval Sing (student looks at music)
1. Play the cadence.
2. Ask the student to sing the ♩ part as you play both the ♩ and ♩ parts.
3. Repeat, playing only the ♩ part as the student sings the ♩ part.

Level 4 Scales

Stop-and-Go Scales

1. Right Hand
   a) What notes does your thumb play? ____ , ____
   b) What note does your 4th finger play? ____

2. Left Hand
   a) What notes does your thumb play? ____ , ____
   b) What note does your 4th finger play? ____

3. Look at Exercise No. 1 below. Fill in the blanks with the correct finger number.

4. Play Exercise No. 1. At each fermata, STOP and say the finger and note name for the next note in the hand that is crossing over or under. For example, in m. 1 pause on beat 3 and say "4 on B♭", referring to the next note in the LH, then continue to the next fermata (beat 4, m. 1).

Basic Patterns

Play 5x times a day, increasing the speed slightly every day or two, at your teacher's direction. Start with Exercises

Nos. 2 & 3. Once you are able to play them solidly at the top speed, move on to Exercises Nos. 4 & 5.

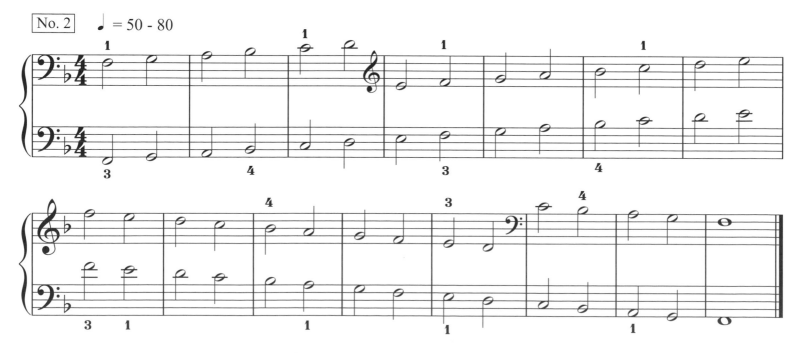

43

No. 3 ♩ = 50 - 80

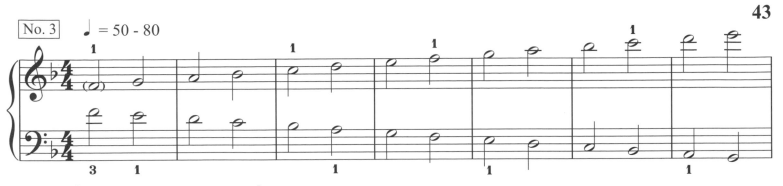

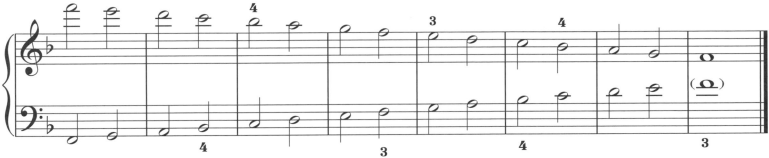

No. 4 ♩ = 40 - 100

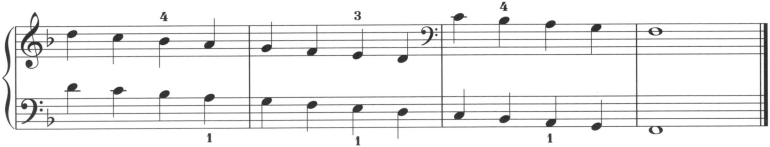

No. 5 ♩ = 40 - 100

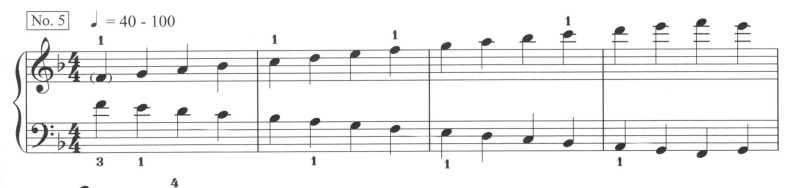

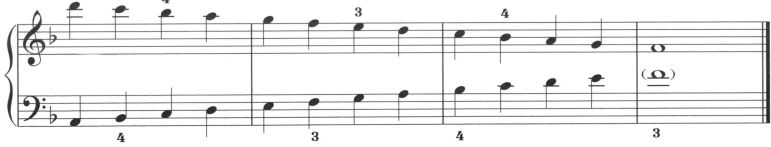

Level 4 Chords

Cadences

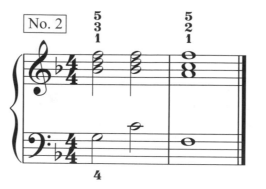

Chords

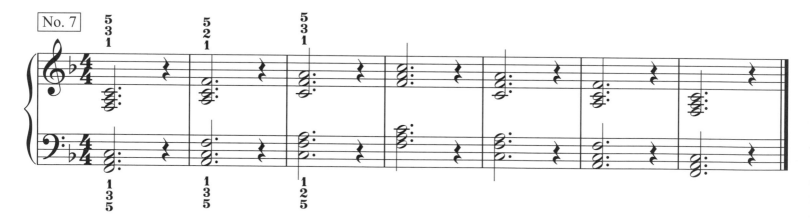

No. 9

No. 10

No. 11

No. 12

Level 4 Arpeggios

No. 1

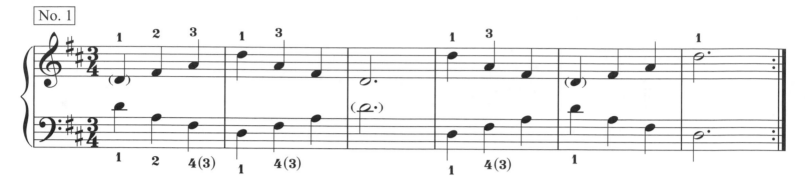

No. 2

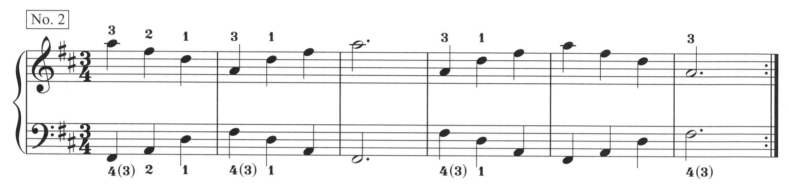

No. 3

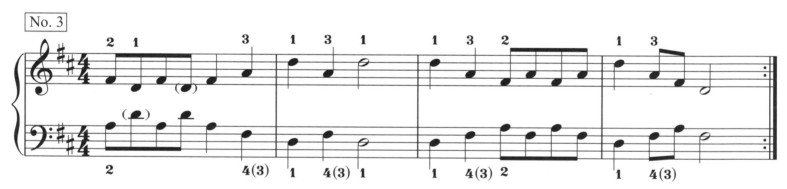

No. 4

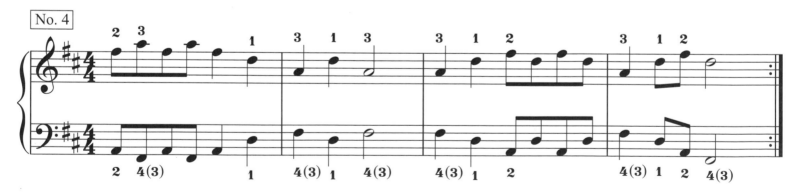

No. 5

Level 4 Blues Scales & Licks

Blues Scales take their name from "blues" notes, which are played at a lower pitch than notes usually found in a major scale. The most common type of Blues Scale uses six notes:

1. Start with a major scale;
2. Leave out the 2nd and 6th scale degrees;
3. Lower the 3rd and 7th scale degrees a half step;
4. Add the note between the 4th and 5th scale degrees.

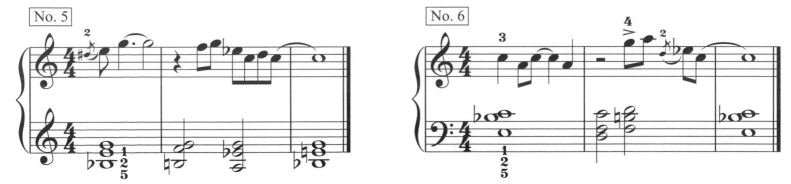

Level 4 Drills

Downstroke Exercises

1. Preparation

a) Rest both fingers on the surface of the keys.
b) Swing "in":
   i. Your arm moves straight up and toward the fallboard;
   ii. Your wrist raises;
   iii. Your fingers remain on the keys or lift very slightly.

2. Sound Production

Swing back "down" into the keys. This downward motion creates the sound. Keep your hand and arm straight – don't let your wrist drop below key level. After striking the keys, fingers relax.

3. Follow Through

Float to cover the next notes, keeping your hand and arm straight.

Upstroke Exercises

1. Preparation

Rest your hand on the surface of the keys.

2. Sound Production

a) Play the first note in each measure with finger motion only.
b) Play the second note by swinging "in". This time, the upward motion creates the sound:
   i. Your arm moves straight up and toward the fallboard;
   ii. Your wrist raises;
   iii. The finger on the second note plays as a result;
   iv. Your other fingers remain on the keys or lift slightly.

Think of it like jumping off a diving board. Your body goes up (represented by the arm and wrist here), the diving board (the piano key) goes down.

3. Follow Through

a) Relax your wrist and arm and return to level position;
b) Float to cover the next notes;
c) Repeat all steps starting with Preparation.

Upstroke / Downstroke Relaxation Exercises

1. Preparation

a) Rest your fingers on the surface of the keys.
b) Swing "in" in preparation for the downbeat:
   i. Your arm moves straight up and toward the fallboard;
   ii. Your wrist raises;
   iii. Your fingers remain on the keys or lift very slightly.

2. Sound Production

a) Swing back "down" into the keys on beat 1 of each measure to play the notes;

b) On beat 2, swing "in" again, keeping the keys down so the sound continues; then release your weight back "down" into the key on beat 3;
c) Repeat step "b" on beats 4 & 5. Note that the initial sound from beat 1 should never be interrupted.

3. Follow Through

On beat 6, swing "in" and up, releasing the keys and moving your hand into position to play the notes in the next measure. Repeat all steps starting with Preparation.

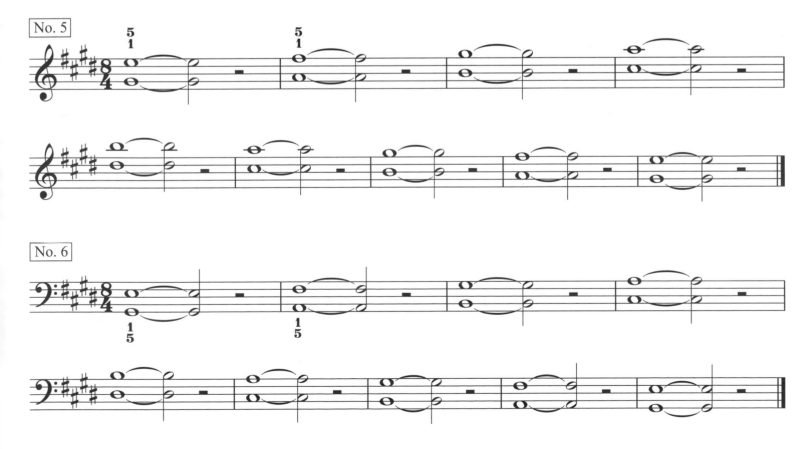

How to Use This Book

The *American Popular Piano Skills* books are designed to be used as a flexible tool for learning the fundamental skills of playing the piano. Research tells us that the most effective way to learn is in small increments, repeated frequently. That's a good thing, considering that many piano students today have very busy schedules and may not have big chunks of time to devote to practice at one time.

How much time should you spend on basic skills? The best choice, of course, is to spend a moderate amount of time daily on technic, sightreading and ear training. But even a smaller amount of time each day, every day is better than spending a lot of time on one day after several days of non-practice.

The Open Plan System

The Open Plan organization of the *American Popular Piano Skills* books encourages skill acquisition at each student's natural pace. Review the chart below to help understand how it works.

How should you schedule assignments of Skills? Progress will vary depending on each student's needs and practice timetable.

- **Faster moving students** can do one module per week.
- **Many students** will work on two or three skill areas within a module each week.
- **Students with less practice time** often do just one skill area.

Areas that need extra work may of course be repeated as necessary.

American Popular Piano
Skills Book-Level Four

Four Learning Units to be done by the student at home		Four Examination Units to be administered by the teacher at the lesson	
Each Unit contains: **4 Learning Modules** Each module covers the following skill areas:		Each Unit contains: **2 Tests** **Midterm:** to be completed after Module 2 **Final:** to be completed after Module 4	
Technic	Chords, arpeggios, blues scales, drills, and scales; along with rhythmic, dynamic, and articulation variants	Technic	Chords Arpeggios Blues Scales Drills Scales
Prepared Sightreading	A short musical excerpt	Sightreading	Short examples, with skills checklist
Aural Skills– Rhythmic	Rhythm clapping in two parts	Aural Skills– Listening	Echo Clap Clap-Along Echo Sing
Aural Skills– Pitch	Interval sing, cadence sing, sing-along	Aural Skills– Reading	Interval Sing

Some Basic Tips

Singing Vocalizing has not always been part of traditional piano lessons. Yet recent research has clearly established its importance for developing crucial listening and audiating skills.

Teaching and learning singing in this context is not hard, but does take patience. Many students have not sung and will need some time and work in order to get comfortable. Stick with it! Studies have shown that even those who seem totally tone-deaf on the first attempt can improve significantly with practice.

- Check that posture is good, breathing deep and even, and throat relaxed.
- If the student is having trouble matching pitch, ask them to sing a note and hold it. Find the same pitch and sing it with them. Then ask them to move their voice with you as you sing to the correct pitch.
- Visual and verbal feedback is crucial. Saying "higher" or "lower", or moving your hand up or down to help them find the pitch is a great help.

Technic Technic should be practiced daily. Vary the focus of each week's assignment using the Technic Box in each Module.

- **Fill in the blanks** for the metronome marking (M.M.) and the number of the exercise.
- **Circle** the chosen key(s), articulation(s), and dynamic(s).

Technical exercises are set out in a single key in the last few pages of this book. For students who work better from a printed page, consider using the *Level 4 Technic Book* for the other keys.

Sightreading The word "sightreading" is a misnomer; a better term might be "pattern recognition" or even "flash learning". A good sightreader recognizes familiar patterns in new arrangments; he or she is able to think ahead, keep going despite mistakes, and keep a steady beat.

Here are some steps that have helped my students improve their sightreading:

- Play the piece at a slow tempo without stopping. After finishing, go back and circle mistakes. This builds both analysis and musical memory skills.
- Play slowly again and try to fix all the mistakes – and not add any new ones!
- Play a third time, counting out loud. This time it should be error free.

Steps may be repeated as necessary.

Mix Do you have to do all the activities for every section? You'll make the right decision based on available time, skill level and long-term goals. Remember, the most important factor in improving fundamentals is: **work on them — and do it often!!**